DevOps for Beginners

A Practical Guide to Automation, CI/CD, and Cloud

Basil U.

COPYRIGHT PAGE

About the Author

Basil is a seasoned software engineer based in Dubai, United Arab Emirates, with over 8 years of experience in developing dynamic web applications for both personal projects and global enterprises.

Throughout his career, Basil has contributed his expertise to a diverse array of companies, ranging from startups to large-scale enterprises. He possesses extensive knowledge in cloud computing, mobile application development, AI integration, API integration, and database management.

I extend my heartfelt gratitude to my family, whose unwavering support has been instrumental in the creation of this book. Special thanks to my wife, Onyi, and our children for their endless encouragement and support.

Content

Chapter One
Introduction to DevOps

What is DevOps?

Imagine you're building a house. You have architects drawing the plans, construction workers assembling the structure, electricians wiring the place, and painters adding the final touch. Now, what if these teams worked in silos, never communicating properly? The result? Delays, costly mistakes, and rework.

In this book, we bring DevOps to life by diving into **real-world scenarios** and hands-on use cases. We'll walk through setting up and managing cloud infrastructure using **AWS EC2**, secure remote access with **PuTTY and PuTTYgen**, and automation with **Bash scripting and Linux commands**.

By the end of this chapter, you will:

- ◼ Know how to launch and connect to an **EC2 instance**.
- ◼ Understand how to use **PuTTY and PuTTYgen** for secure SSH access.
- ◼ Get hands-on experience with **Bash scripting** to automate tasks.
- ◼ Explore essential **Linux commands** used in DevOps workflows.
- ◼ Examine real-world **case studies** showcasing DevOps best practices.
- ◼ Look ahead at **future trends** shaping the **DevOps landscape**.

This is exactly what used to happen in software development before **DevOps** emerged.

DevOps is a combination of **Development (Dev) and Operations (Ops)**. It's a set of **practices, tools, and a cultural shift** that bridges the gap between software developers and IT operations teams. The goal? To streamline the entire software development and deployment process, ensuring fast, reliable, and high-quality software delivery.

But DevOps is more than just a process, it's a **mindset**. It encourages collaboration, automation, and continuous feedback, helping teams build, test, and deploy software faster and more efficiently.

The Evolution of Software Development

Before DevOps, organizations followed the **Waterfall model**, where development happened in distinct, sequential phases:

1. **Planning** – Gathering requirements
2. **Development** – Writing code
3. **Testing** – Checking for errors
4. **Deployment** – Releasing software
5. **Maintenance** – Fixing bugs and making updates

The problem? These phases often took months (sometimes years), and teams worked in isolation. Developers would write code and "throw it over the wall" to operations, who were responsible for deploying it. When issues arose, both teams blamed each other, causing delays and inefficiencies.

Then came the **Agile methodology,** which introduced iterative development and frequent releases. While Agile improved collaboration between developers and business teams, operations were often left out of the loop. This led to the birth of DevOps, integrating both development and operations into a seamless workflow.

Why DevOps Matters

If you've ever experienced slow software updates, buggy applications, or long release cycles, you've encountered the pain points DevOps aims to fix. Let's explore why DevOps is a game-changer:

1. **Faster Software Delivery** – By automating processes and improving collaboration, teams can release updates quickly and efficiently.
2. **Higher Quality Software** – Continuous testing and feedback ensure that code is thoroughly vetted before deployment.
3. **Improved Collaboration** – Developers, operations, and even security teams work together, reducing bottlenecks.
4. **Reduced Failures and Faster Recovery** – Automated testing and monitoring help catch issues early, making it easier to fix them.

5. Scalability and Flexibility – DevOps practices support cloud-native development, enabling businesses to scale applications effortlessly.

The Key Principles of DevOps

DevOps isn't just about tools—it's about adopting key principles that drive efficiency and collaboration. Here are the core concepts:

1. Collaboration and Communication

Breaking down silos between development and operations teams is crucial. This means fostering a culture where everyone shares responsibility for software delivery.

2. Automation

From writing code to deploying applications, automation is at the heart of DevOps. It reduces manual work, minimizes errors, and speeds up development cycles.

3. Continuous Integration and Continuous Deployment (CI/CD)

CI/CD is a DevOps practice where code changes are automatically tested and deployed. This ensures software is always in a release-ready state.

4. Infrastructure as Code (IaC)

Instead of manually configuring servers, teams use code to define infrastructure. This makes deployments more predictable and repeatable.

5. Monitoring and Feedback

Tracking application performance and gathering user feedback allows teams to make improvements continuously.

DevOps vs. Traditional IT Practices

To understand the impact of DevOps, let's compare it to traditional IT approaches

Aspect	Traditional IT	DevOps
Development Speed	Slow, sequential phases	Fast, iterative releases
Collaboration	Siloed teams	Cross-functional teams
Deployment	Manual and error-prone	Automated and reliable
Feedback	Delayed and infrequent	Continuous and real-time
Infrastructure	Manually configured	Defined as code (IaC)

DevOps eliminates inefficiencies and accelerates software delivery by embracing automation and collaboration.

Common DevOps Myths Debunked

As a beginner, you may come across some misconceptions about DevOps. Let's clear them up:

Myth #1: DevOps is Only for Large Companies

Reality: DevOps is beneficial for organizations of all sizes. Whether you're a startup or a multinational corporation, DevOps principles can help improve your software delivery.

Myth #2: DevOps is Just About Tools

Reality: While tools like Docker, Kubernetes, and Jenkins are important, DevOps is primarily about culture, collaboration, and automation.

Myth #3: DevOps Eliminates the Need for IT Operations

Reality: DevOps doesn't replace operations teams—it integrates them into the software development process, making their work more efficient.

Getting Started with DevOps

Now that you understand what DevOps is and why it matters, you're probably wondering: **How do I get started?** Here's a simple roadmap:

Step 1: Learn Version Control (Git & GitHub)

Version control is the foundation of DevOps. It helps track changes, collaborate with teams, and roll back code when needed. Start by learning Git commands and using GitHub for collaboration.

Step 2: Understand CI/CD Pipelines

Learn how Continuous Integration (CI) automated testing and how Continuous Deployment (CD) ensures fast and reliable releases.

Step 3: Get Hands-on with Containers (Docker)

Containers help package applications and their dependencies, making deployment consistent across environments.

Step 4: Explore Infrastructure as Code (Terraform, Ansible)

IaC allows you to define and manage infrastructure using code, ensuring repeatable and scalable deployments.

Step 5: Monitor Applications (Prometheus, Grafana)

Monitoring ensures your applications run smoothly and provides insights into performance and security.

DevOps is revolutionizing the way software is developed and deployed. By fostering collaboration, automation, and continuous feedback, it helps organizations deliver better software faster.

In the next chapter, we'll dive into **DevOps Culture and Collaboration**, where you'll learn how to manage code effectively using Git and GitHub. Get ready to take your first hands-on step into the world of DevOps!

Chapter Two
DevOps Culture and Collaboration

Introduction

DevOps is more than just tools and automation, it is a **cultural shift** that fosters collaboration, transparency, and continuous improvement. A strong DevOps culture empowers teams to break silos, streamline workflows, and deliver high-quality software faster.

In this chapter, we will explore:

- The core principles of DevOps culture
- Breaking down silos between development and operations
- Building a collaborative and high-performing DevOps team
- Best practices for fostering a DevOps mindset

Core Principles of DevOps Culture

A successful DevOps culture is built on **shared responsibility, automation, and continuous learning.** The key principles include:

1. Collaboration and Communication

DevOps bridges the gap between **development (Dev)** and **operations (Ops)** teams. Instead of working in isolation, teams collaborate throughout the software lifecycle, from planning to deployment and maintenance.

2. Continuous Feedback

Fast and **continuous feedback loops** help teams detect and resolve issues early. Monitoring, logging, and real-time analytics ensure teams can respond to incidents quickly.

3. Automation and Efficiency

Automation is at the heart of DevOps culture. From CI/CD pipelines to infrastructure management, automation reduces manual effort and increases efficiency.

4. Embracing Failure as a Learning Opportunity

A strong DevOps culture does not punish failure but treats it as an opportunity to learn and improve. **Blameless post-mortems** encourage teams to analyze failures and prevent future issues.

Breaking Down Silos Between Development and Operations

Traditional software development follows a **waterfall approach**, where development and operations teams work separately. DevOps removes these barriers by promoting:

- **Shared responsibilities** for code quality, security, and infrastructure.
- **Early involvement** of operations teams in development discussions.
- **Cross-functional teams** where developers and operations engineers work together.

Example: Dev and Ops Collaboration in CI/CD

- **Developers** write code and push changes to version control (e.g., GitHub, GitLab).
- **Automated tests** run to validate the code.
- **Operations teams** ensure the infrastructure can support deployment.
- **Monitoring tools** provide feedback on performance and stability.

Building a Collaborative and High-Performing DevOps Team

A DevOps team is built on trust, transparency, and shared goals. Key roles in a DevOps culture include:

- **DevOps Engineers** – Automate processes and maintain CI/CD pipelines.
- **Software Developers** – Write code with deployment and monitoring in mind.
- **Site Reliability Engineers (SREs)** – Focus on uptime, scalability, and performance.
- **Security Engineers** – Ensure security is integrated throughout the process.

Key Traits of a High-Performing DevOps Team

- **Empathy:** Team members understand and respect each other's challenges.
- **Accountability:** Everyone takes responsibility for quality and reliability.
- **Transparency:** Open communication about issues, challenges, and progress.
- **Continuous Learning:** Teams constantly improve through training and knowledge sharing.

Best Practices for Fostering a DevOps Mindset

To cultivate a strong DevOps culture, organizations should:

1. Encourage a Growth Mindset

DevOps thrives on **continuous learning**. Encourage teams to experiment, innovate, and adapt to new tools and practices.

2. Implement Blameless Post-Mortems

When an incident occurs, teams should focus on understanding what went wrong instead of assigning blame. A **blameless post-mortem** fosters learning and improvement.

3. Promote Knowledge Sharing

- Hold **weekly DevOps discussions** to share experiences and challenges.
- Organize **cross-team training sessions** to upskill team members.
- Document **best practices and lessons learned** in a shared repository.

4. Use DevOps Metrics to Drive Improvement

Tracking key DevOps metrics helps teams measure success and identify areas for improvement:

Metric	Description
Deployment Frequency	How often new code is deployed
Lead Time for Changes	Time taken from code commit to production
Mean Time to Recovery (MTTR)	Time taken to resolve incidents
Change Failure Rate	Percentage of deployments that fail

DevOps culture is about **people, processes, and technology working together** to deliver software efficiently and reliably. By fostering collaboration, continuous learning, and automation, organizations can build high-performing DevOps teams.

In the next chapter, we will explore **Version Control and Collaboration**, discussing strategies to implement DevOps at scale in large organizations.

Chapter Three
Version Control and Collaboration

Introduction

Imagine you're working on a software project with a team of developers. Everyone is making changes to the code, but without a structured system to track those changes, things quickly get messy. Code might get overwritten, bugs could be introduced, and debugging becomes a nightmare. This is where **version control** comes to the rescue.

Version control is a fundamental concept in DevOps, enabling teams to track changes, collaborate efficiently, and maintain a history of their work. In this chapter, we'll explore **Git**, the most popular version control system, and **GitHub**, a platform that facilitates team collaboration. By the end of this chapter, you'll have a solid grasp of Git commands, branching strategies, and best practices for working in a team.

What is Version Control?

Version control is a system that records changes to files over time. It allows multiple people to work on the same project without conflicts. If a mistake is made, you can revert to an earlier version instead of starting from scratch.

There are two types of version control systems:

1. **Centralized Version Control (CVCS)** – A single central server stores all versions of the project. Example: Subversion (SVN).
2. **Distributed Version Control (DVCS)** – Every developer has a full copy of the project history. Example: Git.

Git, being a **distributed** system, is the preferred choice in DevOps due to its flexibility, speed, and robustness.

Getting Started with Git

Git is an open-source distributed version control system that allows developers to track changes, collaborate on projects, and maintain a history of their work.

Installing Git

To start using Git, install it on your system:

- **Windows**: Download from git-scm.com and follow the installation wizard.
- **Mac**: Use Homebrew: `brew install git`
- **Linux**: Install via package manager, e.g., `sudo apt install git`

To verify installation, run: `git --version`

Configuring Git

Set up your name and email (required for commit tracking):

```
git config --global user.name "Your Name"

git config --global user.email "your.email@example.com"
```

To check your configuration:

```
git config --list
```

Basic Git Commands

Once Git is installed, you can start using it in your projects.

Initializing a Repository

A repository (repo) is where Git stores your project history.

```
git init
```

This creates a `.git` directory that tracks changes.

Adding and Committing Changes

1. Create a file: `echo "Hello DevOps" > file.txt`
2. Check status: `git status`
3. Add file to staging: `git add file.txt`
4. Commit changes: `git commit -m "Initial commit"`

Viewing History

To see commit history:

```
git log --oneline
```

Branching and Merging

Branching allows you to work on features separately from the main codebase.

Creating a Branch

```
git branch feature-branch
```

Switching Branches

```
git checkout feature-branch
```

Merging Branches

```
git checkout main
git merge feature-branch
```

Deleting a Branch

```
git branch -d feature-branch
```

Working with GitHub

GitHub is a cloud-based platform for hosting and collaborating on Git repositories.

Creating a Remote Repository

1. Sign up on GitHub.
2. Create a new repository.
3. Connect it to your local repository:

```
git remote add origin https://github.com/yourusername/repo.git
git push -u origin main
```

Cloning a Repository

To copy an existing repository:

```
git clone https://github.com/yourusername/repo.git
```

Pulling Latest Changes

```
git pull origin main
```

Best Practices for Git Collaboration

- **Commit Frequently:** Small, meaningful commits help track changes effectively.
- **Write Clear Commit Messages:** Use descriptive commit messages like `fix: corrected login bug`.
- **Use Branching Strategically:** Follow Git Flow or GitHub Flow for structured development.
- **Review Code Before Merging:** Use pull requests and code reviews to maintain quality.

Version control is an essential part of DevOps. Git and GitHub enable seamless collaboration, ensuring projects remain organized and error-free. In the next chapter, we'll dive into **Continuous Integration and Continuous Deployment (CI/CD)**, a key DevOps practice for automating software delivery. Stay tuned!

Chapter Four
Continuous Integration and Continuous Deployment (CI/CD)

Introduction

Imagine you're working on a software project with multiple developers. Each developer writes code on their local machine, but when they merge their changes into the main codebase, errors, conflicts, or integration issues can arise. This slows down development, increases bugs, and delays releases. **Continuous Integration (CI) and Continuous Deployment (CD)** solve this problem by automating code integration, testing, and deployment, ensuring a smooth and reliable development workflow.

In this chapter, we'll break down **CI/CD**, its importance in DevOps, the tools involved, and how you can set up a simple CI/CD pipeline. By the end of this chapter, you'll understand how CI/CD enhances software quality, speeds up releases, and reduces manual work.

What is CI/CD?

Continuous Integration (CI) is the practice of automatically integrating code changes from multiple contributors into a shared repository. It involves running automated tests to catch bugs early.

Continuous Deployment (CD) automates the release of tested code to production environments. In some cases, **Continuous Delivery** refers to preparing the code for deployment, while **Continuous Deployment** means automatically deploying without manual approval.

Why CI/CD Matters in DevOps

- **Faster Development Cycles:** Reduces the time spent merging code and debugging integration issues.
- **Improved Software Quality:** Automated testing catches bugs early.
- **Consistent and Reliable Deployments:** Ensures that code is deployed in a repeatable manner.
- **Less Manual Work:** Developers focus on coding rather than deployment.

CI/CD Pipeline Explained

A **CI/CD pipeline** is an automated sequence of steps that take code from development to production. A typical pipeline consists of the following stages:

1. **Code Commit:** Developers push changes to a version control system (e.g., GitHub).
2. **Build:** The application is compiled and dependencies are installed.
3. **Test:** Automated tests are executed to validate functionality.
4. **Deploy:** The tested code is deployed to production or staging environments.
5. **Monitor:** Logs and metrics are collected to ensure stability.

Popular CI/CD Tools

There are various CI/CD tools available. Some popular choices include:

- **Jenkins:** An open-source automation server.
- **GitHub Actions:** CI/CD workflows integrated into GitHub.
- **GitLab CI/CD:** A built-in pipeline system within GitLab.
- **CircleCI:** A cloud-based CI/CD service.
- **Travis CI:** A cloud-based CI/CD tool for open-source projects.

Setting Up a Simple CI/CD Pipeline

Let's walk through setting up a basic CI/CD pipeline using **GitHub Actions**.

Step 1: Create a GitHub Repository

Ensure your project is hosted on GitHub.

Step 2: Add a CI/CD Workflow

Inside your repository, create a `.github/workflows/ci-cd.yml` file and add the following configuration:

```yaml
name: CI/CD Pipeline
on: [push, pull_request]
jobs:
```

```yaml
build:

  runs-on: ubuntu-latest


  steps:

    - name: Checkout Code

      uses: actions/checkout@v2


    - name: Set Up Node.js

      uses: actions/setup-node@v2

      with:

        node-version: '16'


    - name: Install Dependencies

      run: npm install

      - name: Run Tests

      run: npm test

      - name: Deploy (if tests pass)

      run: echo "Deploying..."
```

Step 3: Commit and Push

Push this configuration to your repository, and GitHub Actions will automatically trigger on every code push.

Step 4: Monitor the Workflow

Navigate to the **Actions** tab in GitHub to monitor the pipeline execution.

Best Practices for CI/CD

- **Commit Frequently:** Small, incremental changes reduce merge conflicts.
- **Automate Tests:** Ensure every change is tested before deployment.
- **Use Feature Flags:** Deploy new features safely without impacting users.
- **Monitor Deployments:** Track logs and performance metrics after deployment.
- **Rollback Mechanisms:** Ensure quick recovery in case of deployment failures.

CI/CD is a crucial DevOps practice that automates integration, testing, and deployment. It enhances collaboration, improves software quality, and accelerates development cycles. In the next chapter, we'll explore **Infrastructure as Code (IaC)**, how to automate and manage infrastructure using code. Stay tuned!

Chapter Five
Infrastructure as Code (IaC)

Introduction

Imagine manually configuring servers, installing dependencies, and setting up environments for each deployment. This process is not only time-consuming but also prone to errors. **Infrastructure as Code (IaC)** solves this by automating infrastructure management using code, ensuring consistency, scalability, and efficiency.

In this chapter, we'll explore IaC, its benefits, popular tools, and a step-by-step guide to implementing it in your DevOps workflow. By the end, you'll have a solid understanding of how to automate infrastructure setup just like software development.

What is Infrastructure as Code (IaC)?

Infrastructure as Code (IaC) is the practice of defining and managing infrastructure, such as servers, databases, and networking—through machine-readable configuration files. Instead of manually setting up resources, you use code to automate provisioning and management.

Why IaC Matters in DevOps

- **Consistency:** Ensures that all environments (development, testing, production) are identical.
- **Speed & Efficiency:** Automates infrastructure setup, reducing deployment times.
- **Version Control:** Allows infrastructure configurations to be tracked and managed in repositories.
- **Scalability:** Easily scale infrastructure up or down based on demand.
- **Reduced Errors:** Eliminates human errors caused by manual setup.

Popular IaC Tools

There are several tools available for Infrastructure as Code, each with its own strengths:

- **Terraform:** A widely used tool for provisioning infrastructure across multiple cloud providers.
- **AWS CloudFormation:** Amazon's IaC tool for managing AWS resources.
- **Ansible:** A configuration management tool that automates application deployment and infrastructure setup.
- **Puppet & Chef:** Tools for managing server configurations and enforcing policies.
- **Kubernetes & Helm:** Used for managing containerized applications and their infrastructure.

How IaC Works

IaC follows a **declarative** or **imperative** approach:

- **Declarative:** Defines the desired state of infrastructure, and the system automatically applies changes to match that state. (e.g., Terraform, CloudFormation)
- **Imperative:** Specifies step-by-step commands to reach the desired infrastructure state. (e.g., Ansible, scripts)

Setting Up a Simple IaC Workflow with Terraform

Let's walk through a basic example of using **Terraform** to create a virtual machine on AWS.

Step 1: Install Terraform

Download and install Terraform from terraform.io. Verify installation:

```
terraform --version
```

Step 2: Define Infrastructure Configuration

Create a file named `main.tf` and add the following configuration:

```
provider "aws" {
  region = "us-east-1"
}
```

```
resource "aws_instance" "example" {

  ami           = "ami-0c55b159cbfafe1f0"

  instance_type = "t2.micro"

}
```

Step 3: Initialize and Apply

Run the following commands:

```
terraform init   # Initialize Terraform

terraform apply  # Apply the configuration
```

Terraform will provision an AWS EC2 instance based on the `main.tf` file.

Step 4: Destroy When No Longer Needed

To clean up resources, run:

```
terraform destroy
```

Best Practices for IaC

- **Use Version Control:** Store IaC scripts in Git repositories.
- **Modularize Code:** Reuse configuration components to simplify management.
- **Automate Testing:** Validate IaC configurations before deployment.

- **Enforce Security Policies:** Use IAM roles and least privilege principles.

- **Monitor and Audit:** Track infrastructure changes using logging tools.

IaC revolutionizes infrastructure management by making it automated, scalable, and error-free. By defining infrastructure in code, teams can quickly spin up environments, ensure consistency, and improve operational efficiency. In the next chapter, we'll dive into **Security in DevOps**, where we'll learn how to track system performance and troubleshoot issues efficiently.

Chapter Six
Security in DevOps

Introduction

Security is a fundamental aspect of DevOps that ensures applications and infrastructure remain protected from threats. By integrating security throughout the development and deployment process, teams can proactively identify vulnerabilities and mitigate risks.

In this chapter, we will cover:

- The importance of DevOps security (DevSecOps)
- Key security principles and best practices
- Common security tools used in DevOps
- Implementing security in CI/CD pipelines

Why Security Matters in DevOps

Security threats continue to evolve, making it essential to embed security into every phase of the software development lifecycle (SDLC). **DevSecOps** integrates security practices into DevOps workflows, ensuring:

- Secure coding standards are followed.
- Vulnerabilities are detected early.
- Compliance requirements are met.
- Automated security testing is part of CI/CD.

Key Security Principles

1. **Shift Left Security** – Security testing is done early in the development lifecycle, rather than waiting until deployment.
2. **Least Privilege Access** – Users and applications should only have the minimum access required.
3. **Encryption** – Data in transit and at rest should be encrypted.
4. **Continuous Monitoring** – Security logs and alerts should be monitored in real time.
5. **Automated Compliance Checks** – Policies should be enforced automatically.

Security Tools in DevOps

Several tools help automate security practices in DevOps:

*   **Static Application Security Testing (SAST):** Scans source code for vulnerabilities.
    *   Examples: SonarQube, Checkmarx
*   **Dynamic Application Security Testing (DAST):** Tests running applications for security issues.
    *   Examples: OWASP ZAP, Burp Suite
*   **Container Security:** Scans container images for vulnerabilities.
    *   Examples: Clair, Trivy

- **Infrastructure as Code (IaC) Security**: Ensures cloud configurations are secure.
    - Examples: Checkov, Terraform Sentinel

Implementing Security in CI/CD Pipelines

Security should be seamlessly integrated into CI/CD workflows. Here's how:

Step 1: Perform Code Scanning in CI

Add a static code analysis tool in the pipeline to detect vulnerabilities.

Example using SonarQube in a GitHub Actions pipeline:

```yaml
jobs:
  security_scan:
    runs-on: ubuntu-latest
    steps:
      - name: Checkout code
        uses: actions/checkout@v2
      - name: Run SonarQube Scan
        uses: SonarSource/sonarqube-scan-action@v1.0.0
        with:
          sonar_host_url: "https://sonarqube.example.com"
```

Step 2: Scan Dependencies

Use tools like **OWASP Dependency-Check** to find security issues in dependencies.

Example for Node.js:

```
npx auditjs check
```

Step 3: Enforce Container Security

Run a container vulnerability scan before deploying.

```
trivy image my-app:latest
```

Step 4: Automate Security Compliance Checks

Use tools like **Checkov** to scan infrastructure as code.

```
checkov -d terraform/
```

Security is not an afterthought in DevOps, it should be an integral part of every stage in development and deployment. By implementing **DevSecOps**, using security tools, and automating security checks, teams can build robust and resilient applications.

In the next chapter, we will explore **Monitoring and Logging**, discussing best practices and automation strategies for software delivery.

Chapter Seven
Monitoring and Logging

Introduction

Once infrastructure and applications are deployed, the next critical step is ensuring their reliability and performance. **Monitoring and logging** help DevOps teams detect and resolve issues quickly, optimize performance, and maintain system health.

In this chapter, we will explore:

- The importance of monitoring and logging
- Key monitoring tools and techniques
- Setting up logging for better troubleshooting
- Best practices for effective monitoring and logging

Why Monitoring and Logging Matter

Monitoring and logging serve distinct but complementary roles in DevOps:

- **Monitoring** tracks system health, performance, and availability in real-time.
- **Logging** records system events, errors, and user activities for debugging and auditing.

Together, they help teams **prevent downtime, optimize resources, and ensure a great user experience.**

Key Monitoring Tools

Several tools provide real-time insights into system health:

- **Prometheus:** A popular open-source monitoring system with time-series data storage.
- **Grafana:** A visualization tool often paired with Prometheus for creating dashboards.
- **Nagios:** Monitors applications, networks, and servers.
- **Datadog:** A cloud-based monitoring and analytics platform.
- **New Relic:** Offers real-time application performance monitoring (APM).
- **AWS CloudWatch:** Monitors AWS cloud resources.

Setting Up Prometheus and Grafana

Step 1: Install Prometheus

```
sudo apt update
sudo apt install prometheus -y
```

Step 2: Install Grafana

```
sudo apt install grafana -y
```

Step 3: Configure Dashboards

- Access Grafana at `http://localhost:3000`
- Add Prometheus as a data source
- Create visualizations to monitor CPU, memory, and network traffic

Logging and Log Management

Logs provide detailed records of system events. Popular log management tools include:

- **ELK Stack (Elasticsearch, Logstash, Kibana)**: A powerful log aggregation and analysis tool.
- **Fluentd**: Collects and routes logs efficiently.
- **Splunk**: A commercial solution for log management and analytics.

Setting Up ELK Stack

Step 1: Install Elasticsearch, Logstash, and Kibana

```
sudo apt install elasticsearch logstash kibana -y
```

Step 2: Configure Logstash to Collect Logs Create a `logstash.conf` file:

```
input {
  file {
    path => "/var/log/syslog"
    start_position => "beginning"
  }
}


output {
  elasticsearch {
    hosts => ["localhost:9200"]
  }
}
```

Run Logstash:

```
sudo systemctl start logstash
```

Monitoring and logging are essential for maintaining high-performing and reliable applications. By implementing tools like Prometheus, Grafana, and the ELK stack, DevOps teams can detect issues early and keep systems running smoothly.

In the next chapter, we will dive into **Containerization with Docker**, exploring best practices for securing infrastructure and applications.

Chapter Eight
Containerization with Docker

Introduction to Containers

In the modern DevOps landscape, containerization has revolutionized software development and deployment. Containers allow developers to package applications along with their dependencies, ensuring consistency across different environments. This approach eliminates the infamous "it works on my machine" problem, making deployments more reliable and efficient.

Containers are lightweight, portable, and efficient, as they share the same OS kernel while running isolated applications. Unlike traditional virtual machines (VMs), which require an entire OS per instance, containers provide process-level isolation, significantly reducing resource overhead.

Key Benefits of Containers:

- **Portability:** Containers run consistently across different environments (development, testing, production).
- **Scalability:** Easily scale applications up or down as needed.
- **Efficiency:** Faster startup times and reduced resource consumption compared to VMs.

- **Consistency:** Ensures that applications run the same way across different deployment environments.

Why Use Docker?

Docker is the most widely used containerization platform, providing a simple way to create, deploy, and manage containers. It abstracts complexities associated with container management and integrates well with DevOps tools and CI/CD pipelines.

Advantages of Docker:

- **Easy Deployment:** Developers can build, ship, and run applications effortlessly.
- **Reproducibility:** Ensures consistent environments across teams.
- **Microservices Support:** Facilitates microservices architecture by allowing independent service deployment.
- **Security and Isolation:** Runs applications in isolated environments, improving security.

Docker enables developers to define application dependencies in a standardized format using **Dockerfiles** and manage multi-container applications using **Docker Compose**.

Creating and Managing Docker Containers

To start working with Docker, install the Docker Engine on your system. Once installed, you can create, manage, and deploy containers using the Docker CLI.

Basic Docker Commands:

1. Verify Docker Installation:

```
docker --version
```

2. Pull an Image from Docker Hub:

```
docker pull nginx
```

   Run a Container:

```
docker run -d -p 8080:80 nginx
```

This command runs an Nginx container in detached mode (-d), mapping port 8080 of the host to port 80 of the container.

3. List Running Containers:

```
docker ps
```

4. Stop a Running Container:

```
docker stop <container_id>
```

5. Remove a Container:

```
docker rm <container_id>
```

6. List All Downloaded Images:

```
docker images
```

Docker allows developers to build and share container images using Dockerfiles.

Writing a Dockerfile and Using Docker Compose

A **Dockerfile** is a script that automates image creation. It defines the base image, dependencies, and commands required to set up an application.

Example Dockerfile for a Simple Node.js App:

```dockerfile
# Use the official Node.js base image

FROM node:14


# Set the working directory in the container

WORKDIR /app


# Copy package.json and install dependencies

COPY package.json .

RUN npm install


# Copy the application files

COPY . .


# Expose port 3000

EXPOSE 3000


# Start the application

CMD ["node", "server.js"]
```

To build and run the container:

```
docker build -t my-node-app .
```

```
docker run -p 3000:3000 my-node-app
```

Using Docker Compose for Multi-Container Applications

Docker Compose allows you to manage multi-container applications with a
simple YAML configuration file (docker-compose.yml).

Example of a **Docker Compose file** for a Node.js app with a MongoDB

```
database:

version: '3'

services:

  app:

    build: .

    ports:

      - "3000:3000"

    depends_on:

      - db

  db:

    image: mongo

    ports:

      - "27017:27017"
```

To start the application:

```
docker-compose up -d
```

To stop and remove the containers:

```
docker-compose down
```

Docker simplifies software deployment by encapsulating applications and their dependencies into lightweight, portable containers. By understanding how to create and manage containers, write Dockerfiles, and use Docker Compose, developers can build efficient, scalable, and reproducible applications.

In the next chapter, we will explore **Orchestration with Kubernetes**, focusing on how to manage containers at scale.

Chapter Nine
Orchestration with Kubernetes

Introduction to Kubernetes

As applications grow in complexity, managing multiple containers manually becomes inefficient. Kubernetes, an open-source container orchestration platform, automates the deployment, scaling, and management of containerized applications. Originally developed by Google and now maintained by the Cloud Native Computing Foundation (CNCF), Kubernetes has become the industry standard for container orchestration.

Why Use Kubernetes?

- **Automated Scaling:** Adjusts resources based on demand.

- **Self-Healing:** Restarts failed containers automatically.

- **Load Balancing:** Distributes traffic efficiently among containers.

- **Declarative Configuration:** Uses YAML manifests to define desired states.

- **Multi-Cloud Support:** Runs across various cloud providers and on-premises environments.

Deploying Applications on Kubernetes

Kubernetes uses a declarative model to define application deployments. The key component is a **YAML configuration file** that specifies how an application should run.

Setting Up Kubernetes

Install **kubectl** (Kubernetes CLI) on your system:

```
curl -LO "https://dl.k8s.io/release/$(curl -L -s
https://dl.k8s.io/release/stable.txt)/bin/linux/amd64/kubectl"
chmod +x kubectl
```

```
sudo mv kubectl /usr/local/bin/
```

1. Set up a local Kubernetes cluster using **Minikube:**

```
minikube start
```

2. Verify the cluster is running:

```
kubectl get nodes
```

Deploying a Simple Application

To deploy an application, create a YAML file (`deployment.yaml`):

```yaml
apiVersion: apps/v1
kind: Deployment
metadata:
  name: my-app
spec:
  replicas: 2
  selector:
    matchLabels:
      app: my-app
  template:
    metadata:
      labels:
        app: my-app
    spec:
      containers:
        - name: my-app
          image: nginx
          ports:
            - containerPort: 80
```

Apply the deployment:

```
kubectl apply -f deployment.yaml
```

Check the status:

```
kubectl get pods
```

Managing Pods, Services, and Deployments

Pods

A **Pod** is the smallest deployable unit in Kubernetes, encapsulating one or more containers.

- View running pods:

```
kubectl get pods
```

- Delete a pod:

```
kubectl delete pod <pod_name>
```

Services

A **Service** exposes a set of Pods as a network endpoint. Example service definition (`service.yaml`):

```yaml
apiVersion: v1

kind: Service

metadata:

  name: my-service

spec:

  selector:

    app: my-app

  ports:

    - protocol: TCP

      port: 80

      targetPort: 80

  type: LoadBalance
```

Apply the service:

```
kubectl apply -f service.yaml
```

Find the service details:

```
kubectl get services
```

Deployments

A **Deployment** manages the lifecycle of Pods and ensures the desired number of replicas are running.

- Scale a deployment:

```
kubectl scale deployment my-app --replicas=4
```

- Update a deployment:

```
kubectl set image deployment/my-app nginx=nginx:latest
```

- Rollback to a previous version:

```
kubectl rollout undo deployment/my-app
```

Helm Charts for Kubernetes

Helm is a package manager for Kubernetes that simplifies deployment by bundling applications into **charts**.

Installing Helm

```
curl -fsSL -o get_helm.sh
https://raw.githubusercontent.com/helm/helm/main/scripts/get-helm-3
chmod 700 get_helm.sh
./get_helm.sh
```

Using Helm Charts

- Search for charts:

```
helm search repo nginx
```

- Install an Nginx chart:

```
helm install my-nginx bitnami/nginx
```

- List installed charts:

```
helm list
```

- Uninstall a chart:

```
helm uninstall my-ngin
```

Kubernetes simplifies the deployment and management of containerized applications. By understanding Pods, Services, Deployments, and Helm Charts, you can efficiently orchestrate applications at scale. In the next chapter, we will explore **DevOps in the Real World:**, ensuring application health and performance.

Chapter Ten

DevOps in the Real World: Case Studies, Challenges, and Future Trends

Case Studies of DevOps Adoption

Case Study 1: Netflix – Pioneering Continuous Delivery

Netflix, one of the earliest adopters of DevOps, revolutionized how software is developed and deployed. By leveraging cloud computing and automation, Netflix created an infrastructure that allows for thousands of daily deployments without service interruptions. Key elements of their DevOps strategy include:

- **Chaos Engineering:** Testing system resilience by deliberately injecting failures.
- **Automated Deployment Pipelines:** Ensuring continuous delivery with tools like Spinnaker.
- **Observability:** Using real-time monitoring and logging to prevent outages.

Case Study 2: Etsy – Overcoming Deployment Bottlenecks

Etsy, an e-commerce platform, faced deployment challenges due to a monolithic infrastructure that led to slow release cycles. By embracing DevOps, Etsy achieved:

- **Deployment Automation:** Moving from bi-weekly releases to multiple daily releases.
- **Infrastructure as Code (IaC):** Using tools like Terraform and Chef for scalable infrastructure management.
- **Blameless Postmortems:** Encouraging a culture of learning from failures instead of assigning blame.

Case Study 3: A Startup's Transformation – Cutting Deployment Time from Weeks to Minutes

A small fintech startup struggled with long development cycles, where deploying new features took weeks. By implementing DevOps practices, they:

- Shifted from manual deployments to **automated CI/CD pipelines**.
- Used **Docker and Kubernetes** for containerized applications, ensuring consistency across environments.
- Adopted **monitoring and alerting** with Prometheus and Grafana to detect issues before they became critical.
- Result: Deployment time was reduced from **three weeks to just a few minutes**.

Common Challenges and How to Overcome Them

1. Resistance to Change

Many organizations resist DevOps due to cultural and operational inertia. Overcome this by:

- **Educating teams on DevOps benefits** and providing training.
- **Starting small** with pilot projects before scaling DevOps practices.
- **Encouraging collaboration** between development and operations teams.

2. Security Concerns

With rapid deployments, security can sometimes be overlooked. Address this by:

- **Integrating security early** in the development lifecycle (DevSecOps).
- **Using automated security scanning tools** like Snyk and SonarQube.
- **Implementing role-based access control (RBAC)** to restrict unauthorized access.

3. Tool Overload

Organizations often struggle with too many DevOps tools. Simplify by:

- **Choosing tools that integrate well** with existing workflows.
- **Focusing on automation** rather than tool complexity.
- **Standardizing** tool usage across teams to reduce confusion.

Future Trends in DevOps

1. AI and Machine Learning in DevOps

AI-driven analytics will play a key role in predictive monitoring, anomaly detection, and automated incident response.

2. Serverless Computing

As organizations move toward serverless architectures, DevOps teams will focus more on managing cloud-based, event-driven applications.

3. GitOps

GitOps extends DevOps principles to infrastructure management, enabling declarative configuration and automated deployment via Git repositories.

4. Low-Code/No-Code DevOps

With the rise of low-code/no-code platforms, DevOps will evolve to support citizen developers by integrating automation and CI/CD workflows.

Final Thoughts and Next Steps for Beginners

DevOps is a journey, not a destination. Here are actionable steps for beginners:

1. **Learn the Fundamentals:** Master version control (Git), CI/CD tools (Jenkins, GitHub Actions), and containerization (Docker, Kubernetes).

2. **Experiment with DevOps Tools:** Set up a personal project with CI/CD pipelines and infrastructure as code.

3. **Engage with the Community:** Join DevOps forums, attend meetups, and contribute to open-source projects.

4. **Gain Hands-on Experience:** Work on real-world projects or seek DevOps internships.

By embracing DevOps, you can improve software delivery, increase collaboration, and enhance operational efficiency. Whether you're an aspiring DevOps engineer or a software developer looking to streamline workflows, DevOps offers limitless opportunities for innovation and growth.

Getting Started with AWS for DevOps: Step-by-Step Guide

Step 1: Create an AWS Account and Set Up Billing

Before using AWS services, you need to create an account and configure the payment method.

1. Go to AWS Console

    ○ Open your browser and visit <u>AWS Management Console</u>.

    ○ Click on "Create an AWS Account" if you don't already have one.

2. Provide Your Details

    ○ Enter your email address, full name, and a strong password.

    ○ Choose "Personal" or "Business" account type.

3. Set Up Payment Method

    ○ Enter a valid credit or debit card. AWS requires a payment method even for the free tier.

    ○ AWS may charge a small amount to verify your card, which is refunded later.

4. Verify Identity

   ○ Enter your phone number to receive a verification code.

   ○ Enter the received code to complete verification.

5. Select a Support Plan

   ○ Choose Basic (Free) unless you need premium support.

6. Sign in to AWS Console

   ○ After your account is created, log in at AWS Console.

aws

IAM user sign in ⓘ

Account ID or alias (Don't have?)

[   ]

☐ Remember this account

IAM username

[   ]

Password

[   ]

☐ Show Password   Having trouble?

[**Sign in**   ]

[Sign in using root user email   ]

Create a new AWS account

aws

Free, on-demand training

Boost your career with
600+ digital courses on
AWS Skill Builder

Learn more >

Click on sign in as root user or use email instead
You should see something like this if successfully log In

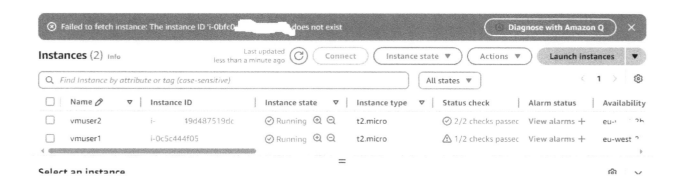

Step 2: Creating an EC2 Instance on AWS

Amazon EC2 (Elastic Compute Cloud) allows you to run virtual servers (instances) on AWS. Follow these steps to create and launch an EC2 instance.

1. Login to AWS Management Console

1. Go to AWS Console.

2. Sign in with your AWS credentials.

3. In the search bar, type "EC2" and select EC2 from the services list.

2. Launch a New EC2 Instance

1. In the EC2 Dashboard, click "Launch Instance".

2. Enter a name for your instance (e.g., "MyDevOpsServer").

3. Choose an Amazon Machine Image (AMI)

An AMI is a pre-configured operating system and software package for EC2.

1. Select an AMI based on your requirements:

   - Amazon Linux 2 (Recommended for most AWS workloads).

   - Ubuntu (Popular for DevOps and cloud-native applications).

   - Windows Server (If you need a Windows-based environment).

2. Click "Select" next to your chosen AMI.

4. Choose an Instance Type

1. AWS offers different instance types based on CPU, memory, and performance.

2. For beginners, select t2.micro (eligible for the AWS Free Tier).

3. Click "Next: Configure Instance Details".

5. Configure Instance Details

1. Keep default settings unless you need a specific configuration.

2. Ensure Auto-Assign Public IP is enabled for internet access.

3. Click "Next: Add Storage".
4. Generate a .pem file to connect to the instance

6. Add Storage

1. The default storage for Amazon Linux 2 and Ubuntu is 8 GB (Free Tier eligible).

2. Increase the size if needed, but note that larger storage incurs additional costs.

3. Click "Next: Add Tags".

7. Add Tags (Optional)

1. Click "Add Tag", then enter:

    -   Key: `Name`

    -   Value: `MyDevOpsServer`

2. Click "Next: Configure Security Group".

8. Configure Security Group

A security group acts as a firewall to control inbound and outbound traffic.

1. Select "Create a new security group".

2. Add rules to allow SSH, HTTP, and HTTPS access:

   - SSH (Port 22): Your IP (for secure access).

   - HTTP (Port 80): Anywhere (for web applications).

   - HTTPS (Port 443): Anywhere (for secure web traffic).

3. Click "Review and Launch".

9. Review and Launch the Instance

1. Verify all settings, then click "Launch".

2. Select an existing key pair or create a new one:

   - If creating a new key pair, download the `.pem` file (this is required for SSH access).

3. Click "Launch Instance".

10. Connect to Your EC2 Instance

Using SSH (For Linux/Mac)

1. Open a terminal and navigate to the `.pem` file location.

Run:

```
chmod 400 your-key.pem
ssh -i your-key.pem ec2-user@your-ec2-public-ip
```

2.
   - Replace `your-key.pem` with your key file name.

   - Replace `your-ec2-public-ip` with your instance's Public IP (found in the EC2 dashboard).

Converting a `.pem` File to a `.ppk` File Using PuTTYgen

PuTTY does not support `.pem` files directly, so you need to convert your `.pem` private key to a `.ppk` file using **PuTTYgen**. Follow these steps:

Step 1: Open PuTTYgen

1. Download and install **PuTTY** (if not already installed) from PuTTY Download Page.

2. Open **PuTTYgen** (it comes with PuTTY).

Step 2: Load the `.pem` File

1. Click on **Load** under the **"Actions"** section.

2. In the file type dropdown (`Files of type`), select **"All Files (.)"** so you can see your `.pem` file.

3. Navigate to the folder where your `.pem` file is stored and select it.

4. Click **Open**.

If you see a confirmation message like *Successfully imported foreign key*, your key has been loaded correctly.

Step 3: Save the .ppk File

1. Click on **Save private key**.

2. If prompted, **choose whether to set a passphrase** for extra security.

   - If you don't want a passphrase, click **Yes** to proceed without one.

3. Choose a folder to save the .ppk file and **give it a name** (e.g., my-key.ppk).

4. Click **Save**.

You now have a .ppk file, ready to use with **PuTTY SSH!**

Using PuTTY (For Windows)

1. Convert .pem to .ppk using PuTTYgen.

2. Open PuTTY, enter the Public IP, and load the .ppk key under SSH > Auth.

3. Click "Open" to connect.

Getting the instance details

1. Click on the instance you want to connect to
2. Locate connect and click on it
3. Look for the SSH tab click on it

Copy your **Public DNS:**

Connect to instance Info

Connect to your instance i-098a   .9dc (vmuser2) using any of these options

EC2 Instance Connect	Session Manager	SSH client	EC2 serial console

Instance ID

📋 i-098a6   : (vmuser2)

1. Open an SSH client.
2. Locate your private key file. The key used to launch this instance is vmuser2.pem
3. Run this command, if necessary, to ensure your key is not publicly viewable.
   📋 chmod 400 "vmuser2.pem"
4. Connect to your instance using its Public DNS:
   📋 ec2-35-17 . -west-2.compute.amazonaws.com

Example:

📋 ssh -i "vmuser2.pem" ec2-user@ec2   :u-west-2.compute.amazonaws.com

ⓘ **Note:** In most cases, the guessed username is correct. However, read your AMI usage instructions to check if the AMI owner has changed the d

Example : ec2-user@ec2-30-100-40-222.eu-west-2.compute.amazonaws.com

Connecting to Your EC2 Instance Using PuTTY (Windows Users)

Step 1: Open PuTTY

1. Launch PuTTY on your computer.

2. In the Host Name (or IP Address) field, paste the Public DNS or Public IP of your EC2 instance.

Step 2: Configure SSH Authentication

1. In the PuTTY Category menu, expand Connection → SSH → Auth.

2. Click Browse and upload your .ppk file (the converted version of your .pem file).

Step 3: Connect to Your EC2 Instance

1. Go back to the Session tab.

2. Click Open to start the SSH connection.

3. If prompted with a security alert, click Accept.

Step 4: Log In to Your Instance (if you use:)
ec2-30-100-40-222.eu-west-2.compute.amazonaws.com

1. When the terminal opens, enter the default username:

   ○ Amazon Linux 2: ec2-user

   ○ Ubuntu: ubuntu

   ○ Debian: admin

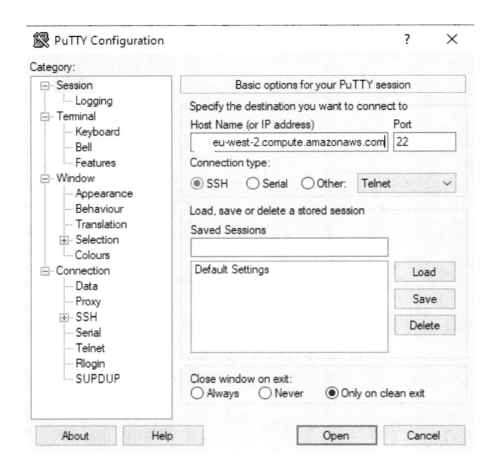

```
ec2-user@vmuser2:~

 Using username "ec2-user".
 Authenticating with public key "imported-openssh-key"
Last login: Mon Mar 24 12:16:10 2025 from            142
       #_
  ~\_  ####_          Amazon Linux 2
 ~~  \_#####\
 ~~     \###|          AL2 End of Life is 2026-06-30.
 ~~      \#/___
  ~~      V~' '->
   ~~~         /       A newer version of Amazon Linux is available!
    ~~._.   _/
      _/ _/            Amazon Linux 2023, GA and supported until 2028-03-15.
    _/m/'                   https://aws.amazon.com/linux/amazon-linux-2023/

9 package(s) needed for security, out of 12 available
Run "sudo yum update" to apply all updates.
[ec2-user@vmuser2 ~]$ ls
autodeploy.log  awsrepo  basil23.s  basil23.sh  basil23.sH  deploy.log  ec2-user@
[ec2-user@vmuser2 ~]$ ls -lrt
total 176
-rw-rw-r-- 1 ec2-user ec2-user   1678 Mar 22 12:24 vmuser2.pem
-rw-rw-r-- 1 ec2-user ec2-user   1674 Mar 22 12:24 vmuser1.pem
-rw-r--r-- 1 root     root       1674 Mar 22 12:35 ec2-user@
-rw-rw-r-- 1 ec2-user ec2-user     10 Mar 22 20:18 basil23.s
-rw-rw-r-- 1 ec2-user ec2-user      0 Mar 22 20:19 basil23.sH
-rwxrwxr-x 1 ec2-user ec2-user      0 Mar 22 20:19 basil23.sh
drwxrwxr-x 2 ec2-user ec2-user     24 Mar 24 12:20 scriptfiles
-rw-r--r-- 1 ec2-user ec2-user     69 Mar 24 16:50 deploy.log
drwxrwxr-x 9 ec2-user ec2-user    307 Mar 24 18:17 awsrepo
-rw-r--r-- 1 ec2-user ec2-user 155567 Mar 27 13:33 autodeploy.log
[ec2-user@vmuser2 ~]$
```

Now that we have launched and connected to our EC2 instance, let dive into scripting

Hands-On with Bash Scripting for Automation

Bash scripting is a powerful way to **automate repetitive tasks** in DevOps, such as **server setup, deployments, backups, and log management**. Instead of manually executing multiple Linux commands, you can write a **Bash script** that runs them automatically.

Example: A Simple Bash Script

```bash
#!/bin/bash
echo "Updating system..."
sudo apt update && sudo apt upgrade -y
echo "Installing Nginx..."
sudo apt install nginx -y
echo "Starting Nginx service..."
sudo systemctl start nginx
```

■ What This Script Does:

1. Updates the system packages.

2. Installs the **Nginx** web server.

3. Starts the Nginx service.

Bash scripting is essential in DevOps for **CI/CD pipelines, infrastructure automation, and server management**

Creating a Simple Bash Script to Display Your Name

Follow these step-by-step instructions to create and execute a Bash script that prints your name on the screen.

Step 1: Create the Script File

Open your terminal and enter the following command to create a new script file named `firstscript.sh`:

bash

```
cat > firstscript.sh
```

- If the file does not exist, `cat >` will create it.

- If the file already exists, this command will overwrite it.

Alternatively, you can use a text editor like nano to create the file:

bash

```
nano firstscript.sh
```

Step 2: Add the Shebang (#!)

The first line of the script should be:

bash

```
#!/bin/bash
```

This line ensures that the script runs using the Bash shell.

Step 3: Add the echo Command

Next, type the following command inside the file to print your name:

bash

```
echo "My Name is Basil"
```

Replace Basil with your actual name.

Step 4: Save and Exit

To exit and save the script:

- If you used `cat >`, press Ctrl + D.

- If you used `nano`:

  1. Press Ctrl + X

  2. Press Y (Yes) to save

  3. Press Enter to confirm

Step 5: Make the Script Executable

Before running the script, give it execution permissions:

bash

```
chmod +x firstscript.sh
```

This command makes `firstscript.sh` an executable file.

Step 6: Verify Execution Permission

To check if the script has execution permission, run:

bash

```
ls -lrt firstscript.sh
```

If the script has execution rights, you will see something like this:

```
-rwxr-xr-x 1 user user 50 Mar 27 10:00 firstscript.sh
```

The x indicates execution permission.

Step 7: Run the Script

Now, run the script by typing:

bash

```
./firstscript.sh
```

It should output:

```
My Name is Basil
```

```
[ec2-user@vmuser2 ~]$ cat > firstscript.sh
#!/bin/bash
echo "My Name is Basil"
[ec2-user@vmuser2 ~]$ chmod +x firstscript.sh
[ec2-user@vmuser2 ~]$ ./firstscript.sh
My Name is Basil
[ec2-user@vmuser2 ~]$
```

A script that accept user name and display it using nano:

```
  GNU nano 2.9.8

#!/bin/bash
echo "Please Enter Your Name"
read name
echo "Your name is $name"
```

```
[ec2-user@vmuser2 ~]$ nano secondscript.sh
[ec2-user@vmuser2 ~]$ chmod +x secondscript.sh
[ec2-user@vmuser2 ~]$ ./secondscript.sh
./secondscript.sh: line 1: !#/bin/bash: No such file or directory
Please Enter Your Name
Basil
Your name is Basil
[ec2-user@vmuser2 ~]$ 
```

Essential Linux Commands for DevOps Workflows

DevOps engineers rely on Linux commands for automation, system management, and troubleshooting. Here are some key commands:

1. File and Directory Management:

    - `ls` → List files and directories

    - `cd` → Change directory

    - `pwd` → Print current directory

    - `mkdir` → Create a new directory

    - `rm -rf` → Delete files or directories

2. File Operations:

    - `cat file.txt` → View file content

    - `nano file.txt` → Edit a file

    - `cp source dest` → Copy files

    - `mv old new` → Rename/move files

3. Permissions and Ownership:

    - `chmod +x script.sh` → Make script executable

- `chown user:group file` → Change file ownership

4. Process Management:

   - `ps aux` → List running processes

   - `kill -9 PID` → Force stop a process

   - `top` → Monitor system performance

5. Networking:

   - `ping google.com` → Check network connectivity

   - `curl -I website.com` → Fetch HTTP headers

   - `netstat -tulnp` → View open ports

6. Package Management:

   - `apt-get install package` (Debian/Ubuntu)

   - `yum install package` (RHEL/CentOS)

7. Logging and Monitoring:

   - `tail -f /var/log/syslog` → Monitor logs in real-time

   - `df -h` → Check disk usage

   - `free -m` → Check memory usage

Take Home Assignment:

1. Write a script that accept user name and age, then display on screen
2. Write a script that runs execution permission on a file
3. Write a script that installs a package
4. Write a script that removes execution permission on a file

Guide to automate file execution

```bash
1    #!/bin/bash
2
3    while true; do
4        echo "Enter File Name you Want to Give Permission:"
5        read filename
6
7        if [ -f "$filename" ]; then
8            echo "Enter the Permission Type to Give $filename (e.g., 755, 644):"
9            read permission
10
11           chmod "$permission" "$filename"
12           echo "Permissions for $filename have been updated to $permission."
13
14       else
15           echo "File '$filename' not found! Please enter a valid file."
16       fi
17
18       echo "Do you want to continue? (yes/no)"
19       read response
20       if [ "$response" != "yes" ]; then
21           break
22       fi
23   done
24
```